Jokes, Riddles and Trivia for Kids Bundle

Over 1000 Different Jokes, Riddles, Brain Teasers and Trivia Questions for Smart Kids

DL Digital Entertainment

TABLE OF CONTENTS BOOK 1

TABLE OF CONTENTS BOOK 2

The Jumbo Jokes and Riddles Book for Kids

Over 500 Hilarious Jokes, Riddles and Brain Teasers Fun for The Whole Family

DL Digital Entertainment
MADE TO ENTERTAIN

DL Digital Entertainment

CHAPTER 1: INTRODUCTION

We would like to personally thank you for taking the time to purchase our book *The Jumbo Jokes and Riddles Book for Kids*. We've spent countless hours putting together only the best, laugh out loud jokes for you, the kids and the family to enjoy! You can expect to find in the first half of this book over 500 jokes put into categories such as knock, knock, silly, food, doctor-doctor, animal, spooky and school. The second half of this book will be focused on Riddles and Brain Teasers These jokes and riddles are guaranteed to make you laugh hard, test your brain and have all kinds of fun with the kids, friends and family!

The Jumbo Jokes and Riddles Book is very versatile thanks for it also being available in audio format on audible.com! Use it on your own before bed, with friends at a get together, with family at the dinner table or camping with relatives; the possibilities with *The Jumbo Jokes and Riddles Book* are endless. Be creative and utilize it to its full potential!

CHAPTER 2: WHY JOKES AND RIDDLES?

This ultimate assortment of jokes for kids, family and friends will not only make you laugh but do so in a fun and interactive way. Jokes have been around since the dawn of time and have many other benefits such as:

-Confidence Boosting: With so many kids and people in general struggling with self-confidence in our day and age, listening and interacting with these jokes and riddles in a safe environment with family and friends gives them the opportunity to comfortably say answers and repeat hilarious jokes and riddles, giving them the ability to not be afraid to express themselves.

-Relieve Stress: Jokes help in relieving your anger, depression, tension and stress and make you feel light and irritation free. It also improves the mood by reducing

anxiety and fear. Laughter increases heart rate and blood pressure, both of which cools down your stress response.

-Improved Bonding: The Jumbo Jokes and Riddles Book is one of the best ways for friends and family to spend time with each other and build positive, healthy relationships through laughter and participation when listening to the jokes and trying to answer the questioning ones.

-Personal Health: Jokes make us laugh and impacts the body in a very positive way. When you start to laugh, it not only lightens your body but also induces many physical changes in it as well. Not only that, but funny jokes boost up the human immune system by increasing infection fighting antibodies.

-Reduce Boredom: Having a book such as The Jumbo Jokes and Riddles Book gives you the ability to have fun and entertainment on demand.

-Develop Humor: Jokes and riddles sharpen your sensibilities and tune our capabilities. It improves your personality by bringing out your lighter side. Humor also allows people to express their feelings without any hesitation.

Now, that's enough talking. Are you ready to get started with *The Jumbo Jokes and Riddles Book.* Awesome! Let's Begin.

CHAPTER 3: KNOCK, KNOCK JOKES

"Laughter is an instant vacation" - Milton Berle

1.Knock, knock!

Who's there?

Leaf

Leaf who?

Leaf me alone!

2. Knock! Knock!

Who's there?

Are two

Are two who?

Are two-D2, of course.

3. Knock, knock!

Who's there?

Ashe

Ashe who?

Bless you!

4. Knock, knock!

Who's there?

Lettuce

Lettuce who?

Lettuce in and you'll find out!

5. Knock, knock!

Who's there?

Hawaii

Hawaii who?

I'm fine, Hawaii you?

6. Knock, knock!

Who's there?

Orange

Orange who?

Orange you going to open the door?

7. Knock, knock!

Who's there?

Tank

Tank who?

You're welcome!

8. Knock, knock!

Who's there?

Who

Who who?

Is there an owl in there?

9. Knock, knock!

Who's there?

Anita

Anita who?

Anita borrow a pencil

10. Knock, knock!

Who's there?

Theodore

Theodore who?

Theodore is stuck and it won't open!

11.Knock, knock!

Who's there?

Sure

Sure who?

Sure would be nice if you opened the door!

12. Knock, knock!

Who's there?

Police!

Police who?

Police! Let us in!

13. Knock, knock!

Who's there?

Amarilly

Amarilly who?

Amarilly nice person!

14. Knock, knock!

Who's there?

Cows go

Cows go who?

Cows don't go who, they go moo!

15. Knock, knock!

Who's there?

Alli

Alli who?

Alligator, that's who!

16. Knock, knock!

Who's there?

Dinosaur

Dinosaur who?

Dinosaurs don't go who, they go ROAR!

17. Knock, knock!

Who's there?

Annie

Annie who?

Annie body going to open the door already?

18. Knock, knock!

Who's there?

Barbie

Barbie Who?

Barbie Q Chicken!

19. Knock, knock!

Who's there?

Frank!

Frank who?

Frank you for being my friend!

20. Knock, knock!

Who's there?

Olive

Olive who?

Olive right next door to you.

21. Knock, knock!

Who's there?

Orange.

Orange who?

Orange you glad I didn't say banana?

22. Knock, knock!

Who's there?

Ice cream

Ice cream who?

Ice cream if you don't let me in!

23. Knock, knock!

Who's there?

Spell.

Spell who?

W-H-O

24. Knock, knock!

Who's there?

Somebody too short to ring the doorbell!

26. Knock, knock!

Who's there?

Abe

Abe who?

Abe C D E F G H...

27. Knock knock!

Who's there

Boo

Boo who?

I didn't mean to make you cry! It's just me!

28. Knock, knock!

Who's there?

Nun

Nun who?

Nun of your business!

29. Knock Knock!

Who's there?

I Love

I Love who?

I don't know, you tell me!

30. Knock Knock!

Who's there?

Bless!

Bless, who?

I didn't sneeze!

31. Knock knock!

Who's there?

Beehive.

Beehive who?

Beehive yourself or you'll get into trouble!

32. Knock knock!

Who's there?

Howard!

Howard who?

Howard I know?

33. Knock! Knock!

Who's there?

Justin.

Justin who?

Justin the neighborhood and thought I'd come over.

34. Knock knock

Who's there?

Mikey!

Mikey who?

Mikey doesn't fit in the keyhole!

35. Knock, knock!

Who's there?

Watson.

Watson who?

Watson the T.V. tonight?

36.Knock knock!

Who's there?

Beets!

Beets who?

Beets me!

37. Knock, knock!

Who's there?

Broccoli!

Broccoli who?

Broccoli doesn't have a last name, silly.

38. Knock knock!

Who's there?

Wooden shoe!

Wooden shoe who?

Wooden shoe like to hear another joke?

39. Knock knock!

Who's there?

Alpaca

Aplaca who?

Alpaca the suitcase, you load the car!

40. Knock knock!

Who's there?

Dishes

Dishes who?

Dishes the police, open up!

41. Knock! Knock!

Who's there?

Kanga.

Kanga who?

Actually, it's kangaroo.

42. Knock! Knock!

Who's there?

Déjà.

Déjà who?

Knock! Knock!

43. Knock! Knock!

Who's there?

A broken pencil.

A broken pencil who?

Nevermind, it's pointless.

44. Knock, knock!

Who's there?

Nobel

Nobel who?

No bell! That's why I knocked

45. Knock! Knock!

Who's there?

Honeybee.

Honeybee who?

Honeybee a dear and open the door, please.

46. Knock! Knock!

Who's there?

Robin.

Robin who?

Robin you — hand over the cash!

47. Knock! Knock!

Who's there?

Interrupting cow.

Interrupting cow....

MOOOO!

CHAPTER 4: SILLY JOKES

"A day without laughter is a day wasted" - Winnie the Pooh

Before getting into these silly jokes, we wanted to let you know that in between the jokes and the answer, we will be providing you with 8 seconds to come up with an answer of your own so you can interact and have as much fun as possible.

Let's get started

1. What did one wall say to the other wall?
Answer: I'll meet you at the corner!

2. Which flower talks the most?

Answer: Tulips of course, because they have two lips!

3. What's a pirate's favorite letter

Answer: Arrrrr!

4. What musical instrument is found in the bathroom?

Answer: A tuba toothpaste!

5. Why are ghosts bad liars?

Answer: Because you can see right through them

6. What do you call a fly without wings?

Answer: A walk!

7. Why do bees have sticky hair?

Answer: Because they use honey combs!

8. What time do you go to the dentist

Answer: At tooth-hurty!

9. What do you get when you cross a snowman with a vampire?

Answer: Frostbite!

10. What has four wheels and flies?

Answer: A garbage truck!

11. Why did the man run around his bed?

Answer: Because he was trying to catch up on his sleep!

12. What's a goblins favorite position playing soccer?

Answer: Ghoul keeper!

13. Why did the golfer wear two pairs of pants?

Answer: Incase he got a hole in one!

14. Where do pencils go for vacation?

Answer: Pencil-vania

15. What did 0 say to 8?

Answer: Nice belt!

16. Why did the gum cross the road?

Answer: It was stuck to the chickens foot!

17. What is brown and sticky?

Answer: A stick!

18. Why did the picture go to jail?

Answer: It was framed!

19. How did Benjamin Franklin feel when he discovered electricity?

Answer: Shocked!

20. What kind of shoes do ninjas wear?

Answer: Sneakers!

21. What do you call a flower that runs on electricity?

Answer: A power plant!

22. What's a tornado's favorite game?

Answer: Twister!

23. What do you call a dinosaur that can't see?

Answer: A Do-you-think-he-saw-us!

24. What did the left eye say to the right eye?

Answer: Between us, something smells!

25. Why couldn't the toilet paper cross the road?

Answer: It got stuck in the crack!

26. Why did the pig go to the kitchen?

Answer: He felt like bakin!

27. What kind of boat goes around a castle?

Answer: A moat-er-boat!

28. What did one plate say to the other?

Answer: Lunch is on me!

29. What do you call a pig that knows karate?

Answer: A pork chop

30. What race is never run?

Answer: A swimming race!

31. What did one volcano say to another?

Answer: I lava you!

32. What is red and goes up and down?

Answer: A tomato in an elevator!

33. Why is basketball such a messy sport?

Answer: Because you dribble on the floor!

34. What can you serve but never eat?

Answer: A tennis ball!

35. What runs but never gets anywhere?

Answer: The oven!

36. Why did the girl eat her homework?

Answer: Because the teacher said it was a piece of cake

37. Why did the girl tip-toe past the medicine cabinet?

Answer: Because she didn't want to wake the sleeping pills!

38. Why did the robber take a bath?

Answer: Because he wanted to make a clean getaway!

39. What did the traffic light say to the car?

Answer: Don't look i'm changing!

40. Why was the Egyptian girl confused?

Answer: Because her daddy was a mummy!

41. What did the blanket say to the bed?

Answer: Don't worry, I've got you covered!

42. What do you call a button that won't unbutton?

Answer: A belly button!

43. What sounds do porcupines make when they kiss?

Answer: Ouch!

Chapter 5: Food Jokes

"There is no love more sincere than the love of food." –
George Bernard Shaw

Before we jump into these food jokes, we wanted to let you know that they will work the same way that the silly jokes did. we will be providing you with 8 seconds to come up with an answer of your own so you can interact and have as much fun as possible.

Let's eat!

1.   When do you stop at green and go at red?
Answer: When you're eating a watermelon!

2. Which part of the day is the easiest to break?

Answer: Breakfast

3. Why did the bread, muffin, cookie and graham crackers go to see a doctor?

Answer: Because they were all feeling crummy

4. What is black; white; green and bumpy?

Answer: A pickle wearing a tuxedo.

5. What do you call cheese that isn't yours?

Answer: Nacho cheese!

6. Did you hear the rumor about the peanut butter?

Answer: I'm not telling you. You might spread it!

7. Why do the French like to eat snails?

Answer: Because they don't like fast food!

8. Why shouldn't you tell an egg a joke?

Answer: Because it might crack up!

9. What can you eat, play with, watch T.V. on and listen to music with?

Answer: Apples

10. Waiter, will my pizza be long?

Answer: No sir, it will be round!

11. What is green and sings?

Answer: Elvis Parsley

12. Why did the banana go to the doctor?

Answer: Because it wasn't peeling very well!

13. What candy do you eat on the playground?

Answer: Recess-Pieces!

14. What do elves make sandwiches with?

Answer: Shortbread!

15. What is a pretzel's favorite dance?

Answer: The Twist!

16. What are twins favorite fruit?

Answer: Pears!

17. What do you give to a sick lemon?

Answer: Lemon-aid

18. Why did the lady love to drink hot chocolate?

Answer: Because she was a cocoa-nut

19. What did lettuce say to celery?

Answer: Quit stalking me!

20. Why are teddy bears never hungry?

Answer: They're never hungry because they are always stuffed!

21. Which vegetable plays sports?

Answer: Squash!

22. What did one potato chip say to the other?

Answer: Shall we go for a dip?

23. Why did the orange stop in the middle of the road?

Answer: Because he ran out juice!

24. What do you call a banana that likes to dance?

Answer: A banana shake!

25. Why did the man get fired from the banana factory?

Answer: Because he kept throwing the bent ones away!

26. Why couldn't the sesame seed leave the gambling casino?

Answer: Because he was on a roll!

27. What's in an astronaut's favorite sandwich?

Answer: Launch meat!

28. Why did the little boy eat as fast as he could?

Answer: He didn't want to lose his appetite!

29. Did you hear what the joke about oatmeal was about?

Answer: A lot of mush

30. What did Mr.Hamburger name his daughter?

Answer: Patty!

31. What does a hot dog say when it gets really hot?

Answer: My buns are starting to burn!

32. What did the little girl call her popsicle when she lost control of it?

Answer: a DROP-sicle!

33. What never uses its teeth to eat anything?

Answer: A comb

34. How did the hipster burn her tongue?

Answer: she sipped her coffee before it was cool!

35. Why are cooks cruel?

Answer: Because they whip cream and beat eggs!

36. What does an evil hen lay?

Answer: Deviled Eggs!

37. What do you get from a pampered cow?

Answer: Spoiled milk!

38. What do sea monsters eat for lunch?

Answer: Fish and ships!

39. How do chickens bake a cake?

Answer: From scratch!

40. What kind of vegetable would you like tonight?

Answer: Beets me!

41. What's the worst vegetable to serve on a boat?

Answer: Leeks!

42. What day do potatoes hate the most?

Answer: Fry-day!

43. What is a scarecrow's favorite fruit?

Answer: Strawberries!

44. What kind of plates do they use in space?

Answer: Flying Saucers!

45. What did the duck say at the restaurant when the waiter brought him the check?

Answer: "I already have a bill!"

46. What fruit can you use to sip on different types of drinks?

Answer: A straw-berry

47. What kind of dessert is the best chef?

Answer: A cookie

CHAPTER 6: DOCTOR, DOCTOR!

"There is nothing in the world so irresistibly contagious as laughter and good humor." - Charles Dickens

Doctor Doctor jokes are some of our favorite jokes here at DL Entertainment! We will be reading them out at a comfortable pace so you can follow along and participate.

Let's get into it!

1. Doctor, doctor I feel like a carrot
    Don't get yourself in a stew!

2. Doctor, doctor i keep seeing double!

Please sit on the couch.

Which one!?

3. Doctor, doctor, I've lost my memory!

When did this happen?

When did <u>what</u> happen?!

4. Doctor, doctor I feel like a needle.

I see your point!

5. Doctor, doctor, what did the x-ray of my head show?

Absolutely nothing!

6. Doctor, doctor i'm becoming invisible!

Yes, I can see you're not all there!

7. Doctor, doctor I snore so loud I keep myself awake.

Sleep in another room then!

8. Doctor, doctor everyone thinks i'm a liar.

I don't believe that!

9. Doctor, doctor I think i'm a bell

Hmm, take these and if it's not better soon, give me a ring!

10. Doctor, doctor people keep ignoring me

Next please!

11. Doctor, doctor what can you give me for this wind?

Here, take this kite!

12. Doctor, doctor you have to help me out!

Certainly. The exit is right over there.

13. Doctor, doctor I feel like a sheep!

Oh that's very baaaaaad

14. Doctor, doctor, I think I need glasses

You certainly do missy, this is the bike store!

15. Doctor, doctor I think im suffering from Deja Vu!

Didn't I see you yesterday?

16. Doctor, doctor have you got something for a bad headache?

Of course! Just take my shoe and hit yourself in the head!

17. Doctor, doctor can I have a second opinion?

Of course, come back tomorrow!

18. Doctor, doctor I think i'm a dog

How long have you felt like this?

Ever since I was a puppy.

19. Doctor, doctor my little boy has just swallowed a roll of film

Well let's just wait and see if anything develops!

20. Doctor, doctor I feel like a dog!

Sit!

21. Doctor, doctor I feel like an apple!

Well, we must get to the core of this.

22. Doctor, Doctor my sister thinks she is a lift!

Well tell her to come in

I can't, she doesn't stop at this floor!

23. Doctor, Doctor I'm boiling up!

Just simmer down!

24. Doctor, Doctor everyone keeps throwing me in the garbage.

Don't talk rubbish.

25. Doctor, Doctor will this ointment clear up my spots?

I never make rash promises!

25. Doctor, Doctor I think I'm a moth=

Get out of the way, your in my light.

26. Doctor, Doctor I keep thinking I'm a mosquito

Go away, sucker!

27. Doctor, Doctor I swallowed a golf ball!

I can see it's a fairway down there!

28. Doctor, Doctor, I feel like a pack of cards.

I'll deal with you later.

29. Doctor, Doctor my son has swallowed my pen, what should I do?

Use a pencil 'till I get there

30. Doctor, Doctor I feel like a pair of curtains

Well pull yourself together then

31. Doctor, Doctor I keep thinking I'm invisible

What?! Who said that?

32. Doctor, Doctor I think i'm shrinking!

Now, settle down. You'll just have to be a little patient.

33. Doctor, doctor, I've got something wrong with my eyes. I keep seeing an insect spinning around my head.

Don't worry, that's just a bug going around

34. Doctor, doctor it hurts when i do this!

Well, don't do that anymore!

CHAPTER 7: ANIMAL JOKES

"The average dog is nicer than the average person." - *Andy Rooney*

Again, with these animal jokes, we will be providing you with 8 seconds to come up with an answer of your own so you can interact and have as much fun as possible.

We hope you enjoy them!

1.   What do you call a cow that eats your grass?
Answer: A lawn-mooer

2. Why do sharks swim in saltwater?

Answer: Because pepper water makes them sneeze

3. What do you call a girl with a frog on her head?

Answer: Lily

4. What did the turkey say to the rooster when he challenged him to a fight?

Answer: "Are you chicken?"

5. Why did the cow cross the road?

Answer: To get to the udder side

6. What did the leopard say after finishing his meal?

Answer: That really hit the spot!

7. Why do fish and reptiles always keep a trim physique?

Answer: Because they always have scales around

8. How did the worm call home?

Answer: Through his Apple phone

9. What do you call a cold dog sitting on a bunny?

Answer: a chili dog on a bun

10. Why did the cow go to New York?

Answer: To watch a moo-sical!

11. What animal always has a buck?

Answer: A deer

12. Why did the lamb cross the road?

Answer: To get to the baaaaarber shop!

13. How does a mouse feel after it takes a shower?

Answer: Squeaky clean!

14. Where do rabbits go to enjoy their breakfast, lunch and dinner?

Answer: IHOP

15. Where do you put barking dogs?

Answer: In a barking lot

16. What do you call a pig that's been arrested for dangerous driving?

Answer: A road hog

17. Where does an elephant pack his luggage?

Answer: In his trunk!

18. What is the smartest insect?

Answer: A spelling Bee

19. What do dogs, chocolate, and trees have in common?

Answer: Bark

20. What do you call an elephant in a phone booth?

Answer: Stuck!

21. What did the duck say to the stand up comedian?

Answer: "You Quack me up!"

22. What did the bird ask for from the doctor?

Answer: A tweetment

23. How many berries did the skunk want to eat?

Answer: a phew

24. What animal should you never trust?

Answer: A cheetah

25. What type of cats like to go bowling?

Answer: Alley cats!

26. Where do hippopotamuses keep their money?

Answer: In the riverbank

27. What's a snake's favorite subject?

Answer: Hissss-tory!

28. Where do cheetahs, lions, jaguars, tigers, cats and pumas go for their school field trip?

Answer: a meow-seum

29. How do the fish, amphibians, reptiles, and birds stay healthy and fit?

Answer: they all eggsercise!

30. How do you make a goldfish old?

Answer: Take away the G!

31. What do you call an exploding monkey?

Answer: a baboom!

32. Why do skunks always celebrate Valentine's Day?

Answer: They are very scent-imental!

33. What's the difference between a car and a bull?

Answer: A car only has one horn!

34. How does a dog stop a video?

Answer: It presses paws!

35. How is a dog like a telephone

Answer: It has a collar ID!

36. How do you catch a squirrel?

Answer: Climb up a tree and act like a nut!

37. Why did the turtle cross the road?

Answer: To get to the shell station!

38. What is the easiest way to count a herd of cattle?

Answer: With a cowculator!

39. What did the sardine call the submarine?

Answer: A can of people!

40. What animal do you think is the best at baseball?

Answer: A bat of course!

41. What bird can lift the heaviest weight?

Answer: A crane

42. What bird can write?

Answer: A pen-guin

43. What does a dog call sandpaper?

Answer: Ruff

44. What fish only comes out at night?

Answer: A starfish!

45. What do you call a mommy cow that just had a calf?

Answer: Decalfinated!

46. What do you call lending money to a bison?

Answer: a buff-a-loan

47. Where are sharks from?

Answer: Finland!

48. What kind of dog always runs a fever?

Answer: A hot dog

49. What do you give a pig with a rash?

Answer: An oink-ment

50. Why did the dinosaur cross the road?

Answer: The chicken wasn't around yet!

51. What did the porcupine say to the cactus?

Answer: Is that you mommy?

CHAPTER 8: SPOOKY JOKES

"The most wasted of all days is one without laughter." - E.E. Cummings

Spooky jokes have always been some of our favorites! You'll get 8 seconds between the joke and answer to interact with them once again.

Have fun!

1. What noise does a witch's breakfast cereal make? Answer: Snap, crack and pop!

2. What do you call two witches who share a room?

Answer: Broom mates!

3. What type of coffee does a vampire drink?

Answer: De-coffin-ated!

4. What is a skeleton's favourite instrument?

Answer: A trombone!

5. What would you get if you crossed a vampire and a teacher?

Answer: Lots of blood tests!

6. Why was the skeleton scared of the rollercoaster?

Answer: He didn't have the guts to do it!

7. Why did the zombie decide to stay in his coffin?

Answer: He felt too rotten to enjoy the day.

8. Why do ghosts hate rain?

Answer: It dampens their spirits.

9. What do you call a witch that lives at the beach?

Answer: A sand-witch!

10. What is a ghost's favorite bedtime story?

Answer: Little Boo Peep!

11. What kind of mistake does a ghost make?

Answer: A boo boo!

12. What is a vampire's favourite fruit?

Answer: Neck-tarines!

13. How can you tell if a vampire has a cold?

Answer: He starts coffin!

14. Who did the monster take to the Halloween dance?

Answer: His ghoul-friend!

15. Why are vampires so unpopular?

Answer: Because they are pains in the neck!

16. What game do young ghosts love?

Answer: Hide and shriek!

17. What do ghosts eat for dinner?

Answer: Spook-etti!

18. Why don't skeletons play music in church?

Answer: Because they have no organs!

19. Which boats do vampires travel in?

Answer: Blood vessels!

20. Why did the skeleton climb a tree?

Answer: Because a dog was after his bones!

21. What do monsters with poor eyesight wear?

Answer: Spook-tacles!

22. How did the vampire race finish?

Answer: Neck and neck!

23. Where does the witch's frog sit?

Answer: On a toadstool

24. How do ghosts go from floor to floor?

Answer: By scare-case!

25. How does a vampire start a letter?

Answer: Tomb it may concern

26. Where do baby ghosts go during the day?

Answer: Dayscare centres!

27. What do you call two witches living together?

Answer: Broommates!

28. Who was the most famous skeleton detective?

Answer: Sherlock Bones!

29. Why is a monster such a messy eater?

Answer: Because it's always goblin!

30. What do skeletons say before eating?

Answer: Bone appetite!

31. What happens when a ghost gets lost in the fog?

Answer: He is mist!

32. What tops off a ghost's ice cream sundae?

Answer: Whipped scream!

33. Do zombies eat popcorn with their fingers?

Answer: No they eat the fingers separately

34. What did one ghost say to the other ghost?

Answer: Do you believe in people!

35. What kind of streets do zombies like the best?

Answer: Dead ends!

36. Why did the ghost pick his nose?

Answer: Because he had boo-gers!

37. What do you do when 50 zombies surround your house?

Answer: Hope it's Halloween!

38. Where did the goblin throw the football?

Answer: Over the ghoul line!

39. What is a Mummy's favorite type of music?

Answer: Wrap!

40. What do you call a little monsters parents?

Answer: Mummy and Deady!

41. Why did the ghost go trick or treating on the top floor?

Answer: He was in high spirits!

42. What sort of books do skeletons like?

Answer: Spine chillers!

43. Where do phantoms mail their letters?

Answer: At the ghost office!

44. Who is the skeleton king of rock and roll?

Answer: Pelvis!

45. Why was the skeleton so thirsty?

Answer: He was bone dry!

CHAPTER 9: SCHOOL JOKES

"A good laugh recharges your battery." - Unknown

Last, but definitely not least, are school jokes! As kids, these were some of our all time favorite so we are sure you'll enjoy them all! 8 seconds will be given between the joke and the answer.

Enjoy!

1. Why did the teacher write the lesson on the windows?

Answer: He wanted the lesson to be very clear!

2. Who is your best friend at school?

Answer: The princi-pal!

3. Why was the students report card wet?

Answer: Because it was below C level!

4. Why did the Cyclops stop teaching?

Answer: Because he only had one pupil!

5. What flies around the school at night?

Answer: The alpha-bat!

6. What letter from the alphabet is found in a cup?

Answer: T.

7. Why did the teacher jump into the pond?

Answer: To test the waters

8. Why do plants hate math?

Answer: Because it gives them square roots!

9. What did the pencil say to the other pencil?

Answer: Lookin' sharp!

10. What is a mathematician's favorite dessert?

Answer: Pi

11. What is a math teacher's favorite season?

Answer: Sum-mer

12. Why did the science book get poor grades?

Answer: It never did it's own work

13. Why did the students take a ladder to school?

Answer: Because they were going to high school!

14. How do you get straight A's?

Answer: Use a ruler!

15. Why did the kids study in the airplane?

Answer: They wanted a higher education!

16. Who's the king of the classroom?

Answer: The ruler!

17. What do librarians take with them when they go fishing?

Answer: Bookworms

18. What is a pirate's favorite subject?

Answer: Arrrrrrt!

19. Why does it take pirates so long to learn the alphabet?

Answer: Because they spend years at C!

20. What did the paper say to the pencil?

Answer: Write on!

21. What's better than a talking dinosaur?

Answer: A spelling Bee!

22. How do bees get to school?

Answer: They take the school buzz!

23. Why didn't the sun go to college?

Answer: Because it already had a million degrees!

24. What is the smartest state?

Answer: Alabama, because it has four A's and one B!

25. Why did the student do multiplication problems on the floor?

Answer: The teacher told her not to use tables!

26. What building has the most stories?

Answer: Libraries!

27. What is an owl's favorite subject?

Answer: Owl-gebra

28. What happened when the teacher tied all the kids shoelaces together?

Answer: They had a class trip!

29. Why did the children eat their homework?

Answer: Because their teacher said it was a piece of cake!

30. Why was the voice teacher so good at baseball?

Answer: Because she had the perfect pitch!

31. What school subject is a witch good at?

Answer: Spell-ing!

32. What becomes smaller when you turn it upside down?

Answer: The number 9!

33. Why did the teacher wear sunglasses?

Answer: Because her students were bright!

34. Why did the music teacher go up the ladder during music class?

Answer: To reach the high notes!

35. What kind of teacher passes gas?

Answer: A tutor!

36. What did the bully have for lunch?

Answer: A knuckle sandwich!

37. Why was the music teacher not able to open his class room?

Answer: Because his keys were in the piano!

38. Why is history the sweetest lesson?

Answer: Because it's full of dates!

39. Why was the broom late for school?

Answer: He over swept

40. Why did the students study in the airplane?

Answer: They wanted to get higher grades!

41. What do you call a square that's been in an accident?

Answer: A Wreck-tangle!

42. Why did the M&M go to school?

Answer: To become a smartie!

43. Why did the square and triangle go to the gym?

Answer: To stay in shape!

44. What did the glue say to the teacher?

Answer: "I'm stuck on you!"

CHAPTER 10: PUNNY PUNS

"We don't laugh because we're happy, we're happy because we laugh." – William James

1. What did one toilet say to the other?

Answer: You look a bit *flushed*

2. Why was the king's army too tired to fight?

Answer: Too many sleepless knights

3. What do you call a boy named Lee that no one talks to?

Answer: Lonely

4. Why did the spider go to the computer?

Answer: To check out his website

5. Where do polar bears vote?

Anwer: The north pole

6. In what way are cards like wolves?

Answer: They come in packs

7. What do you get when you cross a snake and a pie?

Answer: A python

8. What was the reporter doing at the ice cream shop?

Answer: getting the scoop!

9. What do baseball players eat their food on?

Answer: Home plates

10. Why couldn't the pirate figure out how to play with the cards?

Anwer: He was sitting on the deck!

11. How do you fix a tomato that is broken?

Answer: Just use some tomato paste!

12. Why did the shark spit out the circus clown?

Answer: Because he tasted funny

13. What is purple and 5000 miles long?

Answer: The grape wall of China

14. Did you hear about the guy whose whole left side was cut off?

Answer: He's all right now

15. Why was the calendar so popular back in high school?

Answer: Because it always had dates!

16. What kind of car does Mickey Mouse's wife drive?

Answer: A Minnie van!

17. What kind of joke always gets a reaction?

Answer: A chemistry joke

18. Why do bicycles always fall over?

Answer: Because they are two tired

19. What part of a car is the laziest?

Answer: the wheels since they are always tired...

20. What did the sick elevator say to the other?

Answer: I might be coming down with something

21. Why can't your finger be 12 inches long?

Answer: Then it would be a foot!

22. How do turtles talk to each other?

Answer: They use a shell-phone!

23. Why don't you ever see dragons during the daytime?

Answer: Because they are always fighting knights!

24. What was the brooms excuses for oversleeping on its first day of work?

Answer: "I over swept!"

25. What do you call a knight that's afraid to fight?

Answer: Sir-Render!

26. What did the judge say to the skunk when it walked into the court room?

Answer: Odor in the court!

27. How do you get a tissue to dance?

Answer: You put a little boogie in it

28. Where do polar bears keep their money?

Answer: A snow bank!

29. What did the cheerleader say to the ghost?

Answer: Show some more spirit!

30. What do you call a fake piece of spaghetti?

Answer: an im-pasta!

31. What do you call an old snowman?

Answer: Water

32. Why are concerts always cool inside?

Answer: they are always full fans

33. What did the old man say when he walked into the bar?

Answer: Ouch!

34. What do you call a monkey that likes Durritos?

Answer: A chipmonk

35. Why do shoemakes always go to heavan?

Answer: Because they have perfect souls!

Now, here are one liner puns for your enjoyment!

1. The best way to talk to a fish is to drop them a line
2. A chicken crossing the road is poultry in motion
3. The marine biology seminars weren't for entertainment, but were created for educational porpoises.
4. A skunk fell in the river and stank to the bottom.
5. Energizer Bunny arrested -- charged with battery.
6. In the winter my dog wears his coat, but in the summer he wears his coat and pants.
7. He bought a donkey because he thought he might get a kick out of it.
8. As a scarecrow, people say I'm outstanding in my field.

9. I told my friend 10 jokes to get him to laugh. Sadly, no-pun-in-10-did

10. NASA asked me to organize a party for them. They simply told me to planet.

CHAPTER 11: RIDDLES

1. The man who invented it, doesn't want it. The man who bought it, doesn't need it. The man who needs it, doesn't know it.

Answer: a Coffin

2. I am so simple, that I can only point yet I guide people all over the world.

Answer: Compass

3. Light as a feather, there's nothing in it, but the strongest man can't hold it much more than a minute.

Answer: A breath

4. I cannot speak but I have great knowledge. I'm not a tree but I have leaves. I have hinges but I am neither a door nor a window. What am I?

Answer: a book

5. What goes up as rain comes down?

Answer: an Umbrella

6. Pearl white chest without key or lid. Inside of which golden treasure is hidden. What am I?

Answer: Egg

7. We are twins, We are close together, But we will not touch, But far apart, We become one. What are we?

Answer: Eyes

8. If you feed it, it lives, If you water it, it dies!

Answer: Fire

9. They have not flesh nor feathers, nor scales nor bones; but they do have fingers and thumbs of their own. What are they?

Answer: Gloves

10. The king of it is a happy man, For twelve others he rules with pride. It is one of the world's most beautiful things, But when cold causes suffering and strife. It's vital to everyone, both you and me. Without it, our lives would be lost. It's given away in many forms, But more often at a very high cost. Taken for granted by the mindless, at best. Most difficult to mend, an arduous task, But if you succeed sincerely, you can conquer all the rest.

Answer: Heart

11. I reflect the light, that's not very bright, I sit in the

same place all year, all the time, right here, you cannot see me all right.. at least when it's not night.

Answer: Moon

12. Lovely and round, I shine with pale light, grown in the darkness, a lady's delight.

Answer: Pearl

13. I am blue, red, and many other colors, I have no end, and no gold to find, look for me after a storm or looking at a waterfall. I am green, and have no warts, live not in water, and not on land, some might call me witch's stew parts but I know that I would taste rather bland.

Answer: Rainbow

14. I have no top or bottom but I can hold Flesh, bones and blood all at the same time.

Answer: Ring

15. What gets wetter as it dries?

Answer: Towel

16. What has teeth but cannot bite?

Answer: Comb

17. What five-letter word becomes shorter when you add two letters to it?

Answer: Short

18. What word begins and ends with an E but only has one letter?

Answer: Envelope

19. What has a neck but no head?

Answer: Bottle

20. Which letter of the alphabet has the most water?

Answer: C

21. What starts with a P, ends with an E and has thousands of letters?

Answer: Post Office

22. What begins with T ends with T and has 'T' in it?

Answer: Teapot

23. During what month do people sleep the least?

Answer: February - the shortest month of them all!

24. A cowboy rode to an inn on Friday. He stayed two

nights and left on Friday. How could that be?

Answer: His horse is named Friday

25. Mr. Smith has 4 daughters. Each of his daughters has a brother. How many children does Mr. Smith have?

Answer: He has 5 children, all of the daughters have the same 1 brother.

26. What goes up and down without moving?

Answer: a Staircase

27. I am taken from a mine and shot up in a wooden case, from which I am never released, and yet I am used by almost everybody. What am I?

Answer: Pencil lead

28. What goes up the chimney when down, but cannot go

down the chimney when up?

Answer: An umbrella

29. What is it that has a bottom at the top of them?

Answer: Your legs

30. As I went across the bridge, I met a man with a load of wood which was neither straight nor crooked. What kind of wood was it?

Answer: Sawdust

31. The first man is the master of priceless gems; The second man is the master of love; The third man is the master of shovels; The fourth man is the master of big sticks; Who are they?

Answer: The kings in a deck of cards

32. What instrument can you hear but never see?

Answer: Your voice. You can sing with your voice like an instrument and hear it, but no one can see it; not even you.

33. A house has four walls. All of the walls are facing south, and a bear is circling the house. What color is the bear?

Answer: The house is on the North Pole, so the bear is white.

34. In a one-story pink house, there was a pink person, a pink cat, a pink fish, a pink computer, a pink chair, a pink table, a pink telephone, a pink shower– everything was pink!

What color were the stairs?

Answer: Not pink. It is a one-story house!

35. What is always in front of you but cannot be seen?

Answer: The future

36. Through wind and rain I always play, I roam the earth, yet here I stay; I crumble stones, and fire cannot burn me; Yet I am soft- you can gouge me with your hand.

Answer: The ocean

37. Where can you find cities, towns, shops and streets but no people?

Answer: A map

38. This old one runs forever, but never moves at all. He has not lungs nor throat, but still a mighty roaring call. What is it?

Answer: A waterfall

39. I am not alive, but I grow; I don't have lungs, but I need air; I don't have a mouth, but water kills me. What am I?

Answer: fire

40. A word I know, six letters it contains, remove one letter, and twelve remains. What am I?

Answer: Dozens

41. With thieves I consort, With the vilest, in short, I'm quite at ease in depravity; Yet all divines use me, And savants can't lose me, For I am the center of gravity!

Answer: Letter 'V'

42. What bedtime question can you never answer yes to?

Answer: Are you asleep yet?

43. You can see nothing else, when you look in my face, I will look you in the eye, and I will never lie.

Answer: your reflection

44. What English word retains the same pronunciation, even after you take away four of its five letters?

Answer: Queue

45. I have keys but no doors, I have space but no rooms, I allow you to enter but you are never able to leave. What am I?

Answer: A keyboard

46. You cannot see me, nor can I be touched, you cannot feel me, but I can cook your lunch!

Answer: A microwave plate

47. After booming and zapping is when I emerge, to bring you bright dazzling beauty when I diverge. Some say that I hide enormous wealth, but those riches have always proven stealth. What am I?

Answer: A rainbow

48. I have wings, I am able to fly, I'm not a bird yet I soar high in the sky. What am I?

Answer: An Airplane

49. If four people can repair four bicycles in four hours, how many bicycles can eight people repair in eight hours?

Answer: 16

50. I am used in most sports, have four main holes, come in many different colors and there is a state that shares my name. What am I?

Answer: a Jersey

51. I am a fruit, I am a bird and I am also a person. What am I?

Answer: A kiwi

52. What time did the tooth fairy show up to get a kid's tooth and leave a dollar under the pillow?

Answer: Exactly at TWOoth o'clock

53. What kind of food does the baby chicken make when it goes to the bathroom?

Answer: Chickpeas

54. What vegetable is the king of rock and roll?

Answer: Elvis Parsley

55. What did the doctor prescribe to the sick lemon?

Answer: Lemon-Aid

56. What kind of fruit do computer nerds love the most?

Answer: Macintosh

57. One day, a bean fell in love with some water. The water said they could get married if the bean became used as a flavoring agent. The bean replied that they could get married only if they lived in a colder climate. They agreed and had a baby who happened to be a good rapper. What did they name their baby?

Answer: Vanilla Ice

58. I always try my best to keep up with mustard and bbq sauce. Who am I?

Answer: ketchup

59. What do you call a cat who has sprouted fins and loves to swim?

Answer: Catfish

60. What do golfers drink?

Answer: Iced Tea

CHAPTER 12: CONCLUSION

Wow! You made it through all 500 of the hilarious jokes and mind twisting riddles in this book.... How did they go? Did you have fun? These jokes have all been hand picked in order to make you laugh like there's no tomorrow! We hope you enjoyed going through them and they created some great memories between you, your friends and your family.

Once again, we would like to thank you for reading our book *The Jumbo Jokes and Riddles Book* and we can't wait to hear what you thought about it. If you enjoyed listening to this book, please don't forget to leave a review and let us know exactly how much you loved it. Reviews mean the world to us and help us continue to create books just like this one for years to come.

Thank you!

 DL Digital Entertainment

Trivia Questions for Smart Kids

Over 300 Questions About Animals, Bugs, Nature, Space, Math, Movies and So Much More (Part 1)

DL Digital Entertainment

INTRODUCTION

We would like to personally thank you for taking the time to purchase our book *Trivia for Smart Kids Pt. 1.* We have spent countless hours putting together only the best and most interesting trivia questions for you, the kids and the entire family to enjoy! You can expect to find 250+ different trivia questions ranging from categories such as: Math, History, Geography, Animals, Bugs, T.V. Shows, Movies, Nature, Science and Sports. These trivia questions are guaranteed to make you and your kids think hard and have all kinds of fun while doing so.

Trivia for Smart Kids Pt. 1 is very versatile thanks to being in audio format as well on Audible.com! Use it on your own before bed, with friends at a get together, with family at the dinner table or camping with relatives; the possibilities with it are endless. Be creative and utilize it to its full potential!

WHY TRIVIA QUESTIONS?

This amazing assortment of trivia questions will test not only test your children, but you and your family members in a fun and interactive way. The act of Trivia has been around since the dawn of time and has many other benefits such as:

-Confidence Boosting: With so many kids and people in general struggling with self-confidence in our day and age, doing these trivia questions in a safe environment with family and friends gives them the opportunity to comfortably say answers, even though they might be wrong, allowing them to not be afraid to express themselves.

-Improved Bonding: Trivia For Smart Kids is one of the best ways for friends and family to spend time with each other and build positive, healthy relationships through teamwork and encouragement when trying to solve the

trivia questions found in this book.

*-**Reading Comprehension Skills:** Trivia Questions are often times written in slightly more challenging words and phrases in order to test the listener and make them think. Having children listen to them throughout this book significantly helps improve their reading skills and comprehension.*

*-**Reduce Boredom:** Having an audiobook such as Trivia For Smart Kids gives you the ability to have fun and entertainment on demand. Since we provide it in audiobook form, you can utilize it in any situation you can think of!*

*-**Improve Concentration:** Children - and many adults - suffer from losing focus often and not being able to concentrate for long periods of time. These Trivia questions will force you to put 100% of your focus into them in order to come up with solutions to them, sufficiently boosting overall personal concentration and focus levels.*

Now, that's enough talking. Are you ready to get started with *Trivia For Smart Kids?*

Awesome! Let's Begin.

ANIMAL TRIVIA

"If having a soul means being able to feel love, loyalty and gratitude, then animals are better off than a lot of humans" - James Herriot

1. Which of the following dogs is the smallest?

    A) Dachshund

    B) Poodle

    C) Pomeranian

    D) Chihuahua

    Answer: D, The smallest dog breed is the chihuahua

2. What color are zebras?

A) White with black stripes.

B) Black with white stripes.

C) Both of the above.

D) None of the above.

Answer: B, Zebras have a black base with white stripes.

3. What is the biggest animal on our planet?

A) Blue whale

B) African elephant

C) Giraffe

D) Gray Whale

Answer: A, the Blue Whale is the largest animal currently on the planet

4. Which of the following animals sleep standing up?

A) Gorillas

B) Flamingos

C) Camels

D) Ravens

Answer: B, Flamingos sleep standing up because the salt flats they live on are too caustic to sit down in.

5. What is the fastest water animal?

A) Porpoise

B) Sailfish

C) Flying fish

D) Tuna

Answer: B, The sailfish is the fastest water animal, reaching speeds up to 68 miles per hour.

6. Which of the following animal groups does a zebra belong to?

A) Horse

B) Dog

C) Cat

D) Rat

Answer: A, Zebras belong to the horse family.

7. How many teeth are baby horses born with?

A) 2

B) 10

C) 6

D) 0

Answer: D, baby horses teeth don't show up until about a week after birth

8. Gorillas live in groups called:

A) Squads

B) Gangs

C) Troops

D) Crews

Answer: B, They live in groups called Troops

9. What are baby meerkats called?

A) Katlets

B) Moogs

C) Meeks

D) Pups

Answer: D, baby meerkats are called pups

10. When a baby great white shark is born, how long does it stay with its mother?

A) 1 month

B) 6 months

C) Immediately

D) 1 year

Answer: C, It leaves immediately

11. What is the typical lifespan of a great white shark?

A) 10 years

B) 20 years

C) 30 years

D) 40 years

Answer: C, 30 years

12. On average, how long do lions spend eating each day?

A) 15 minutes

B) 1 hour

C) 2 hours

D) 5 hours

Answer: B, they spend about 1 hour eating each day
eating

13. What is the correct name for an adult female horse?

A) Filly

B) Mare

C) Colt

D) Lon

Answer: B, They are called a Mare

14. Elephants walk quite slowly, approximately 4 mph, but
how fast can they run if they are excited or scared?

A.   20 mph
B.   30 mph
C.   40 mph
D.   50 mph

Answer: B, 30 mph is the speed elephants can run at

15. Us humans have just two sets of teeth in our lifetime but a shark continuously produces new teeth and 'sheds' old teeth throughout its life. How many teeth might a shark grow, use and then shed each year?

A.   60 teeth
B.   600 teeth
C.   6000 teeth
D.   10 teeth

Answer: C, 6000 teeth, this is why fossilized sharks are extremely common.

16. How many different species of fish are there?

A.   310
B.   2100
C.   27000
D.   100000

Answer: C, there are 27000 different species of fish to date!

17. How much water can a fully grown rhinoceros drink per day?

A.   100 litres
B.   1000 litres
C.   500 litres
D.   50 litres

Answer: A, A fully grown rhino can drink up to 100 litres of water per day.

18. On average, how much does a fully grown adult elephant weigh?

A.   1 ton
B.   2 tons
C.   5 tons
D.   0.5 tons

Answer: B, a fully grown elephant weighs approximately 2 tons

19. Which of these animals walks like a camel?

A.   Giraffe
B.   Dog
C.   Cat
D.   Elephant

Answer: A, Giraffes and camels walk by moving both legs on one side and then both legs on the other side!

20. What birds eyes are larger than its brain?

A.   Eagle
B.   Owl
C.   Ostrich
D.   Parrot

Answer: C, Ostrich's eyes are larger than their brains

21. Which animal can look two ways at the same time?

A.   Chameleon
B.   Lizard
C.   Snake
D.   Tortoise

Answer: A, The chameleon has the ability to look two ways at one time

22. What are a moles main source of food?

A.   Lady bugs
B.   Ants
C.   Snails
D.   Earthworms

Answer: D, earthworms are a moles main source of food

23. What is the name for a group of frogs?

A.   Troops
B.   Squad
C.   Army
D.   Force

Answer: C, a group of frogs is called an army

24. What is a fox's den called?

A.   Home
B.   Shelter
C.   Cave
D.   Earth

Answer: D, A foxes den is really called 'Earth'

25. Walt Disney's famous deer was named what?

A.   Lily
B.   Ariel
C.   Nala
D.   Bambi

Answer: D, The famous deer was named Bambi.

26. Which animal has rectangular pupils?

A.   Horse
B.   Deer
C.   Goat
D.   Llama

Answer: C, A goat has rectangular pupils, how crazy is that?!

27. What is the largest land going animal?

A.   Giraffe
B.   Elephant

C.   Moose
D.   Rhino

Answer: B, The largest land animal is the elephant.

28. What animal pollinates banana plants in the wild?

A.   Bees
B.   Flies
C.   Bats
D.   Hummingbirds

Answer: C, surprisingly enough, bats pollinate banana plants in the wild!

29. Which one of these animals can freeze without dying?

A.   Frogs
B.   Birds
C.   Turtles
D.   Fish

Answer: A, a number of studies have shown that frogs can live through being frozen…

30. What is the name for the study of animals?

A.   Entomology
B.   Biology
C.   Mammalogy
D.   Zoology

Answer: D, Zoology is the study of animals

31. What is the correct number for the amount of living species that have been identified?

A.   More than 10 million
B.   More than 100 million
C.   More than 1 million
D.   More than 50 millions

Answer: C, More than 1 million living species of animals have been identified during our time spent on earth

32. One of the characteristics that makes an "animal" and animal is that it:

A.   Is mobile during at least one phase of its life
B.   Has fur, claws, paws, fins, or blubber

C.   Can manufacture its own food through the processing of organic or inorganic material

D.   Has four limbs or more

Answer: A, It has to be able to move about under its own power (be mobile) during a stage of its life, unlike plants and fungi.

BUG AND INSECT TRIVIA

1. How do bees communicate with one another?

A.   Talking
B.   Dancing
C.   Flying
D.   Buzzing

Answer: B, Bees communicate by something called a Waggle Dance

2. On a common ladybug, what color are the spots?

A.   Orange
B.   Red
C.   White
D.   Black

Answer: D, The spots on a common ladybug are black

3. Of these four bugs, which one has teeth?

A.   Flies
B.   Mosquitos
C.   Beetles
D.   Bees

Answer: B, yes, mosquitos have tiny teeth used to cut through skin and even protective layers of clothing

4. How many people do stinging insects send to the emergency room every year?

A.   500
B.   30000
C.   200000
D.   More than 500000

Answer: D, 500,000 or more people get sent to the ER for anything from fire ants to wasps and yellow jackets which can all cause dangerous allergic reactions.

5. Insects make up:

A.   Only a small group of the world's creatures

B.   Most of the world's creatures

C.   A group of creatures that only live in tropical regions

D.   A moderate percentage of the world's creatures

Answer: B, Insects make up the majority of our world's creatures (roughly 70 - 80%!)

6. Insects have at least:

A.   Four legs

B.   Eight legs

C.   Six legs

D.   Two legs

Answer: C, to be considered an insect, they must have 6 legs or more!

7. What does the monarch butterfly do in the winter time?

A.   Flies to warm places

B.   Stays near oceans and coastal regions

C.   It always stays in tropical regions

D.   It flies north

Answer: A, the monarch butterfly seeks out warm places during the winter time

8. The legs of an insect are joined to its:

A.   Head
B.   Abdomen
C.   Both abdomen and thorax
D.   Thorax

Answer: D, Insects legs are always joined to it at their thorax

9. The three insect body parts include:

A.   Head, neck, abdomen
B.   Head, thorax, abdomen
C.   Head, abdomen, tail
D.   Head, body, tail

Answer: B, An insects 3 main body parts are its head, thorax and abdomen

10. Which of the following is not considered an insect and better considered a bug?

A.   Grasshopper
B.   Butterfly
C.   Beetle
D.   Centipede

Answer: D, centipedes have too many legs to be considered an insect

11. Which of the following insects has not evolved much from its original form?

A.   Cockroach
B.   Dragonfly
C.   Dung Beetle
D.   Ant

Answer: A, Fossil records show that insects existed 390 million years ago. Some of the earliest insects, such as cockroaches, have changed very little.

12. What body part do insects us to sense things?

A.   Thorax
B.   Antennae
C.   Wings
D.   Exoskeleton

Answer: B, Insects use their antennae to sense the world around them!

13. Insects do indeed have eyes. What is the main purpose of them?

A.   Detecting colors
B.   Detecting light
C.   Detecting smell
D.   Magnifying images

Answer: B, The simple eyes, or ocelli, are located on the head between the compound eyes. The ocelli aren't used for vision, but to detect changes in the intensity of light.

14. Which body part do insects not share the same as humans?

A.   Heart
B.   Feat
C.   Esophagus
D.   Lungs

Answer: D, On insects, a system of branching air tubes, or tracheae, reaches all parts of the body. Air enters through openings called spiracles.

15. What percentage of insects are harmful to plants and animals?

A.   10 percent
B.   4 percent
C.   2 percent
D.   30 percent

Answer: C, Less than 2 percent of all insect species are harmful; but among them, they can cause major crop damage and spread serious diseases.

16. Which of the following is a sign that an insect is probably safe to eat?

A.   Hairy body
B.   Dull coloration
C.   Long antennae
D.   Has wings

Answer: B, A general rule of thumb is not to eat any brightly colored insects since it's nature's way of warning predators that this insect is poisonous.

17. The term "bug" describes a certain type of insect. What do bugs have that other insects don't have?

A.   Ridges on all six legs
B.   Compound eyes
C.   Piercing and sucking mouthparts
D.   Antennae

Answer: C, bugs have piercing and sucking mouthparts

18. What kinds of insects makes up 40% of described insects?

A.   Bees
B.   Beetles
C.   Mosquitos
D.   Lady Bugs

Answer: B, Beetles make up 40% of described insects!

19. Crickets are famous for chirping, but how do they

make that noise?

A.   Rubbing their legs together
B.   Whistling through their mandibles
C.   Jumping into the air
D.   Rubbing against each other

Answer: A, Crickets make their signature noise by rubbing their legs together.

20. What is the biggest insect ever discovered?

A.   The Giant Weta
B.   The hercules Beetle
C.   The Madagascar Walking Stock
D.   The Dung Beetle

Answer: A, The Giant Weta is the biggest insect ever discovered. It looks like a mixture between a giant cricket and a spider!

21. What insect is the fastest runner?

A.   Dung Beetle
B.   Fire Ant

C.   Harvester Ant
D.   Cockroach

Answer: D, The cockroach is the fastest running insect

22. What is the name for the middle segment of an insects body?

A.   Abdomen
B.   Phalange
C.   Thorax
D.   Antennae

Answer: C, the thorax is the middle region of an insects body

23. Insects live all over the world. What is the only continent where insects do not live?

A.   Australia
B.   Antarctica
C.   Asia
D.   Canada

Answer: B, it is much too cold for insects to live and thrive in antarctica

24. Butterflies taste with their:

A.   Wings
B.   Feet
C.   Antennae
D.   Eyes

Answer: B, Surprisingly enough, butterflies taste things with their feet!

25. Dung beetles roll their turd balls:

A.   In a straight line
B.   1 foot left, then 1 foot right
C.   1 foot left then back 1 foot, then straight
D.   2 feet left and 2 feet right

Answer: A, Dung beetles roll them primarily straight and never according to exact measurement

26. How many stomachs to ants have?

A.   4

B.   6
C.   1
D.   2

Answer: D, ants have 2 stomachs; one to hold the food for itself and the other stomach for fellow ants!

27. Crickets are considered _____ in some parts of the world

A.   Good luck
B.   Bad luck
C.   Money
D.   Evil

Answer: A, in the far east and well across Europe, it is considered very bad luck to kill a cricket, even by accident and considered good luck to see one.

28. Which mosquitoes are the ones that feed on blood?

A.   Male
B.   Female
C.   Brown
D.   Red

Answer: B, Female mosquitoes are the only ones in the family to feed on blood

29. What is a baby grasshopper called?

A.   Hopper
B.   Youngin
C.   Larva
D.   Nymph

Answer: D, Baby grasshoppers are called Nymphs

30. 'Bee Killer' refers to what kind of insect?

A.   Spider
B.   Wasp
C.   Fly
D.   Ant

Answer: C, flies are referred to as 'Bee Killer's'

31. Where are cricket's ears located?

A.   Head

B.   Feet
C.   Front legs
D.   Rear abdomen

Answer: C, Crickets ears are surprisingly found on the front legs! How interesting...

T.V. AND MOVIE TRIVIA

"Movies touch our hearts, and awaken our vision, and change the way we see things. They take us to other places. They open doors and minds. Movies are the memories of our lifetime, we need to keep them alive." - *Martin Scorsese*

1. In the movie 'Toy Story' to whom does Woody belong?

A.   Andy
B.   Sid
C.   Buzz
D.   Billy

Answer: A, Woody belonged to Andy in the Toy story movies

2. In the movie 'Peter Pan' who is Captain Hook's pirate-buddy?

A.   Smee
B.   Big Chef
C.   Peter
D.   Tink

Answer: A, Smee is the little chubby pirate who Hook bosses around.

3. In the movie 'Aladdin' who does Jasmine meet in the marketplace?

A.   Her father
B.   The genie
C.   Her mother
D.   Aladdin

Answr: D, Jasmine and Aladdin meet for the first time when she sneaks out to the marketplace.

4. In the movie 'The Little Mermaid' what is Ariel's little fish friend's name?

A.   Chip
B.   Flounder
C.   Sebastian

D.   Eric

Answer: B, Flounder is Ariel's little yellow fish buddy.

5. Which of these is NOT one of the seven dwarves in Snow White?

A.   Sleepy
B.   Dopey
C.   Bashful
D.   Smiley

Answer: D, The seven dwarves were: Doc, Sneezy, Dopey, Bashful, Grumpy, Sleepy, and Happy.

6. In the TV show 'Catdog' what are Dog's favorite foods?

A.   Tacos with hot sauce
B.   Hot dogs with ketchup
C.   Fish with tartar sauce
D.   Vegetables with cheese sauce

Answer: A, Dog eats the super hot tacos and sauce and then Cat has to suffer!

7. Who lives in a pineapple under the sea?

A.   Catdog
B.   The wild Thornberrys
C.   Doug
D.   Spongebob SquarePants

Answer: D, Spongebob SquarePants lives in a pineapple under the sea!

8. On the show 'Sabrina the Teenage Witch' what is the name of Sabrina's cat?

A.   Salem
B.   Blackie
C.   Warlock
D.   Helga

Answer: A, Salem is a warlock who was turned into a cat and can't change back.

9. In the movie 'Annie', what is Annie's dog's name?

A.   Sandy
B.   Rover
C.   Champion
D.   Lady

Answer: A, Annie names him Sandy because he's the color of sand.

10. On the cartoon 'Recess' who is the ruler of the playground?

A.   Prince Will
B.   King Bob
C.   King Dave
D.   Gus

Answer: B, King Bob was the supreme ruler of the playground!

11. In the movie 'ET' what does Elliot dress up ET as for Halloween to get him out of the house without his Mom seeing?

A.   A ghost with clown feet
B.   A monster with boots
C.   A hunchback with sneakers
D.   A skeleton with no feet

Answer: A, They put a sheet over ET and clown shoes on his feet. Elliot's Mom thinks ET is Gertie, but he's not!

12. What is the name of the show that has these characters on it? Slippery Soap, Paprika, and Magenta.

A.   Gullah Gullah Island
B.   Barney
C.   Eureka's Castle
D.   Blue's Clues

Answer: D, Blue's Clues has these characters on it!

13. Who is Franklin's Friend who is hungry almost all the time?

A.   Snail
B.   Beaver
C.   Bear
D.   Fox

Answer: C, Bear is always hungry in the show Franklin!

14. What were the little people called in "Willy Wonka and the Chocolate Factory"?

A.   Dwarfs
B.   Oompa-Loompas
C.   Munchkins
D.   Fidgets

Answer: B, The little people in the movie were called Oompa-Loompas.

15. In which 2001 movie did Eddie Murphy play the character Donkey?

A.   Shrek
B.   The Lion King
C.   Lilo & Stitch
D.   Tarzan

Answer: A, He played Donkey in Shrek.

16. What movie sequel about a mouse was released in 2002?

A.   Lilo & Stitch

B.   Ice Age
C.   Stuart Little 2
D.   Scooby-Doo

Answer: C, Stuart Little starred a mouse and his child companion George

17. What's the title of the original animated movie about a time when the Earth was overrun by glaciers?

A.   The Emperor's New Groove
B.   Ice Age
C.   The Powerpuff Girls Movie
D.   Toy Story

Answer: B, Ice Age was based around the time that Earth was overrun by glaciers.

18. In which 2001 movie did John Goodman voice the character the big blue not-so-mean monster, Sulley?

A.   Monsters, Inc.
B.   An American Tale
C.   Happy Feet
D.   Toy Story

Answer: A, Monsters, Inc. was the movie that featured John Goodman's Character Sulley

19. In "Land Before Time II" and "V" what character did Littlefoot and his friends see a lot?

A.   The Two Threehorn Twins
B.   Chomper
C.   Monster
D.   Lee

Answer: B, Littlefoot and his friends always seemed to see Chomper.

20. Where was it that the Grinch stole Christmas from?

A.   Whoville
B.   Whereville
C.   Whatville
D.   Whosland

Answer: A, Whoville is where the Grinch stole Christmas from.

21. What film features the animated characters Lola and

Lenny?

A.   Shrek
B.   Ice Age
C.   Finding Nemo
D.   Shark Tale

Answer: D, the animated movie Shark Tale Features Lola and Lenny

22. Which film is about the son of a gangster shark boss?

A.   Are we there yet?
B.   Bee Movie
C.   Shark Tale
D.   Cars

Answr: C, Shark tale is about this!

23. What magical creatures lead Merida to a witch in 'Brave'?

A.   Goblins
B.   Will O' The Wisps
C.   Ghosts

D.   Selkies

Answer: B, Will O' The Wisps were the magical creatures that lead Merida to a witch.

24. Who voiced Remy in 'Ratatouille'?

A.   David Cross
B.   Will Ferrell
C.   Adam Sandler
D.   Patton Oswalt

Answer: D, Patton Oswalt voiced Remy

25. What's the name of the ball with a star that appears in many Pixar films?

A.   Bouncers
B.   Andy's Ball
C.   The Luxo Ball
D.   The BNL Ball

Answer: C, the ball is called the Luxo ball!

26. What fraternity does Mike Wazowski join in 'Monsters University'?

A.   Roar Omega Roar
B.   Oozma Kappa
C.   Alpha Scarems
D.   Sigma Fear Omega

Answer: B, The fraternity Mike joins is called Oozma
Kappa

27. In The Incredibles, before he became Syndrome, he
wore rocket boots and called himself what?

A.   Incrediboy
B.   Incredikid
C.   Rocket Boy
D.   The Incredible Boy

Answer: A, Syndrome became known as Incrediboy

28. Who famously said, "To Infinity and Beyond" in Toy
Story?

A.   Andy
B.   Mr. Potato Head
C.   Rex
D.   Buzz Lightyear

Answer: D, Buzz Lightyear was a spaceman toy in Toy Story and famously said, "To Infinity and Beyond".

29. Who voiced Lightning McQueen in 'Cars'?

A.   Andy Samberg
B.   Ben Stiller
C.   Matt Damon
D.   Owen Wilson

Answer: D, Owen Wilson Voices Lighting McQueen. "Cah chow!"

30. On what planet was Wall-E stranded at the beginning of the movie 'Wall-E'?

A.   Saturn
B.   Mars
C.   Earth
D.   Venus

Answer: C, Wall-E was stranded on planet earth

31. In "Finding Nemo", who states that they have short term memory loss but still remembers some things?

A.   Crush
B.   Nemo
C.   Gill
D.   Dory

Answer: D, Dory is the one in "Finding Nemo" who has the bad memory

GEOGRAPHY TRIVIA

"Without geography, you're nowhere" - Unknown Author

1. Which country is Paris the capital of?

A.   Spain
B.   Canada
C.   France
D.   India

Answer: C, Paris is located in the country of France in Europe

2. What is the national capital city of Canada?

A.   Washington D.C.
B.   Ottawa
C.   Vancouver
D.   Seattle

Answer: B, Ottawa, located in the province of Ontario

3. What's the earth's largest continent?

A.   Antarctica
B.   Asia
C.   Europe
D.   North America

Answer: B, Asia is Earth's largest continent at approximately 17,300,000 square miles (44,806,812 sq km).

4. What razor-thin country accounts for more than half of the western coastline of South America?

A.   Ecuador
B.   Peru
C.   Bolivia
D.   Chile

Answer: D, Chile has a thin coastline of 2650 miles (4265 km) which accounts for more than half of the western coastline of South America.

5. What country has the most natural lakes?

A.   Australia
B.   India
C.   Germany
D.   Canada

Answer: D, Canada has more than half of all the natural lakes in the world.

6. What is the driest place on Earth?

A.   Sahara Desert
B.   Osoyoos, British Columbia
C.   Mcmurdo, Antarctica
D.   Death Valley, California

Answer: C, The driest place on Earth: the McMurdo Dry Valleys in Antarctica. Fun fact: It hasn't rained there for more than 2 million years!

7. Which African nation has the most pyramids?

A.   Egypt
B.   Sudan

C.   Algeria
D.   Libya

Answer: B, Sudan is home to over 200 pyramids

8. What African country served as the setting for Tatooine in Star Wars?

A.   Ethiopia
B.   Cape Town
C.   Gabon
D.   Tunisha

Answer: D, Tatooine was filmed in Tunisha, Africa

9. What is the oldest active volcano on Earth?

A.   Mt. Fuji
B.   Mt. Baker
C.   Mt. Yasur
D.   Mt. Etna

Answer: D, Mount Etna in Italy is thought to be the world's oldest active volcano.

10. What city is the capital of Australia?

A.   Sydney
B.   Canberra
C.   Perth
D.   Melbourne

Answer: B, Canberra replaced Melbourne as the capital of Australia in 1908

11. What is the deepest point in Earth's oceans?

A.   Mariana Trench
B.   Tonga Trench
C.   Eurasian Basin
D.   Java Trench

Answer: A, The deepest part of the ocean is the Mariana Trench

12. What is the smallest state in the USA?

A.   Texas
B.   Idaho
C.   Washington

D.   Rhode Island

Answer: D, Rhode Island is the smallest state in the USA.

13. What is the largest state in the USA by area?

A.   Alaska
B.   Texas
C.   California
D.   Arizona

Answer: A, Alaska is the biggest state by area in the USA

14. Where is the famous rock mural Mt. Rushmore located in the USA?

A.   North Dakota
B.   South Dakota
C.   Arizona
D.   Washington

Answer: B, Mt. Rushmore is located in South Dakota

15. What is the capital of Florida?

A.   Tampa Bay
B.   Miami
C.   Orlando
D.   Tallahassee

Answer: D, Tallahassee is the capital city of Florida, U.S.A.

16. What Australian city boasts the world's largest natural harbor?

A.   Melbourne
B.   Brisbane
C.   Perth
D.   Sydney

Answer: D, Sydney surrounds the world's largest natural harbor.

17. What is the largest country in the world in terms of land area?

A.   United States
B.   Russia
C.   India
D.   Mexico

Answer: B, Russia is the largest country in the world, covering more than one eighth of Earth's inhabited land area.

18. What is the longest mountain range in the world?

A.   Andes
B.   Rocky Mountains
C.   Transantarctic Mountains
D.   Himalayas

Answer: A, The Andes of South America is the longest mountain range in the world, stretching for an estimated distance of 7,000 km (4,350 miles).

19. What is the largest body of water in the world?

A.   Pacific Ocean
B.   Indian Ocean
C.   Arctic Ocean
D.   Atlantic Ocean

Answer: A, The biggest body of water in the world is the Pacific Ocean at 161.8 million km^2 (squared)

20. What is the smallest country when measured by total land area?

A.   Tuvalu
B.   Vatican City
C.   Maldives
D.   Monaco

Answer: B, Vatican City is the smallest country in the world

21. The United Kingdom is comprised of how many countries?

A.   6
B.   8
C.   4
D.   5

Answer: C, The United Kingdom is comprised of 4 different countries.

22. The biggest desert in the world is:

A.   Arabian
B.   Great Australian
C.   Sahara
D.   Namib

Answer: C, The Sahara Desert is the largest desert in the world

23. How many great lakes are there located in Canada and the USA?

A.   2
B.   5
C.   3
D.   7

Answer: B, there are 5 lakes: Superior, Huron, Michigan, Erie and Ontario

24. Which is the world's highest mountain?

A.   Everest
B.   Kilimanjaro
C.   K2
D.   Makulu

Answer: A, Mt. Everest is the highest mountain in the world located in Nepal

25. Which river flows through the Grand Canyon?

A.   Nile River
B.   Colorado River
C.   Missouri River
D.   Yukon River

Answer: B, The Colorado River runs through the Grand Canyon

26. What is the capital city of Spain?

A.   Barcelona
B.   Madrid
C.   Granada
D.   Seville

Answer: B, Madrid is the capital of Spain with a population of 3.3 million people

27. What is the total height of Niagara Falls?

A.   125 feat
B.   57 feat
C.   312 feat
D.   167 feet

Answer: D, Niagara Falls stand at 167 feet tall at the highest point!

28. Who owns the land of Antarctica?

A.   USA
B.   Canada
C.   Russia
D.   None of the above

Answer: D, No one owns the land of Antarctica.

29. Which Italian city is famous for its canals?

A.   Rome
B.   Venice
C.   Florence
D.   Milan

Answer: B, Venice is known for being built on water and having canals as its 'streets'.

30. What are the only two countries to have a land border with the US?

A.   Canada and Mexico
B.   Canada and Cuba
C.   Canada and Spain
D.   Mexico and Brazil

Answer: A, Canada is located above the USA and Mexico is below on a map.

HISTORY TRIVIA

"The more you know about the past, the better prepared you are for the future" - Theodore Roosevelt

1. World War I began in which year?

A.   1925
B.   1919
C.   1914
D.   1945

Answer: C, WWI began shortly after the assassination of Arch-Duke Ferdinand in 1914.

2. Adolf Hitler was born in which country?

A.   Croatia
B.   Slovenia
C.   Germany

D.   Austria

Answer: D, Hitler was born in Lintz, Austria near the German border.

3. In what city was John F. Kennedy assassinated in?

A.   Washington
B.   Dallas
C.   Austin
D.   Miami

Answer: B, JFK was assassinated while driving through Dallas in November 1963.

4. When did the Cold War officially end?

A.   1889
B.   1990
C.   1989
D.   1979

Answer: C, The cold war officially ended in 1989

5. Published after her death, what did teenager Anne Frank leave behind?

A.   A dress
B.   A diary
C.   A bow
D.   A List

Answer: B, Anne Frank left behind a diary

6. Who was the first President of the United States?

A.   George Washington
B.   John Adams
C.   Barrack Obama
D.   Donald Trump

Answer: A, George Washington was the first person to be named president of the United States in 1789.

7. What influential person became President of South Africa in 1994?

A.   Christopher Columbus
B.   Martin Luther King Jr.

C.   Nelson Mandela

D.   Michelangelo

Answer: C, Nelson Mandela became president of South Africa in 1994

8. Whose exploration of the New World had its quincentenary (500 year anniversary) in 1992?

A.   Marco Polo

B.   Christopher Columbus

C.   Ferdinand Magellan

D.   James Cook

Answer: B, Christopher Columbus

9. This famous Civil Rights Movement leader is famous for a speech that starts with "I have a dream..." - what is their name?

A.   Malcolm X

B.   Abraham Lincoln

C.   Martin Luther King Jr.

D.   Rosa Parks

Answer: C, "I have a dream," was the beginning of a

speech by Martin Luther King Jr. which he delivered in 1963 for people to hear

10. Which 4 president's faces can be found at Mt. Rushmore?

A.   George Washington, Jimmy Carter, Abraham Lincoln and Franklin D. Roosevelt
B.   Theodore Roosevelt, Franklin D. Roosevelt, Ronald Reagan, George Bush
C.   Richard Nixon, John F. Kennedy Jr., Bill Clinton, Thomas Jefferson
D.   Thomas Jefferson, George Washington, Theodore Roosevelt, and Abraham Lincoln

Answer: D, The presidents carved into Mount Rushmore are Thomas Jefferson, George Washington, Theodore Roosevelt, and Abraham Lincoln.

11. When did the American Civil War take place?

A.   1961 - 1965
B.   1900 - 1904
C.   1861 - 1865
D.   1856 - 1860

Answer: C, The American Civil War took place 1861 - 1865.

12. What was the Mayflower and what did it carry?

A.   A train with English Immigrants
B.   A ship carrying English Separatists
C.   A flower that symbolized something important
D.   A plane that flew around the world

Answer: B, The Mayflower was the ship that carried English Separatists to the New World now known as America

13. Who was the Prime Minister of Britain during World War II?

A.   Donald Trump
B.   Clement Attlee
C.   Franklin D. Roosevelt
D.   Winston Churchill

Answer: D, Attlee took over from Churchill after the war. He was only the second Prime Minister to be a member of the Labour Party.

14. Who was the leader of the U.S.S.R. during World War II?

A.   Emperor Hirohito
B.   Joseph Stalin
C.   Emperor Akihito
D.   Vladimir Lenin

Answer: B, While Lenin was the first Communist leader of Russia, Stalin served as their leader during World War II

15. Who were the ancient people responsible for building the pyramids?

A.   American people
B.   British people
C.   Egyptian people
D.   European people

Answer: C, The Egyptians built the great pyramids in Egypt

16. In which town was Jesus born?

A.   Paris
B.   Bethlehem
C.   Amsterdam
D.   Washington

Answer: B, Jesus was born in the town of Bethlehem

17. What are the Wright brothers famously known for?

A.   Flying the first powered aircraft
B.   Driving the first powered car
C.   Creating the first powered boat
D.   Building the first powered train

Answer: A, the Wright brothers flew the first powered aircraft on December 17th, 1903.

18. Which country was the first one to use paper money?

A.   Egypt
B.   China
C.   Switzerland
D.   Denmark

Answer: B, China first used paper money during the Tang Dynasty in A.D. 618-907.

19. Who invented the light bulb?

A.   Thomas Edison
B.   Isaac Newton
C.   Abraham Lincoln
D.   Winston Churchill

Answer: A, Thomas Edison invented the light bulb in 1879

20. Alexander Graham Bell invented which of the following devices?

A.   Telephone
B.   Airplane
C.   Car
D.   Train

Answer: A, he invented the telephone in 1876

21. Which city was divided by a wall from 1961 to 1989?

A.   Rome
B.   London
C.   Berlin
D.   Munich

Answer: C, The famous Berlin Wall was enforced on the people of Berlin from 1961 to 1989.

22. Which US Apollo mission was the first to land on the moon?

A.   11
B.   13
C.   10
D.   9

Answer: A, Apollo 11 was the first spaceflight to land humans on the moon.

23. Who was the first man on the moon?

A.   Buzz Aldrin
B.   Neil Armstrong
C.   Alan Shepard
D.   Tim Allen

Answer: B, Neil Armstrong was the first man on the moon on July 16th, 1969.

24. Who drafted the Declaration of Independence?

A.   Abraham Lincoln
B.   George Washington
C.   Neil Armstrong
D.   Thomas Jefferson

Answer: D, Thomas Jefferson drafted the document and it was published in July of 1776.

25. In which country were the modern Olympic Games held for the first time?

A.   Spain
B.   Greece
C.   Florence
D.   London

Answer: B, Greece was the first place to hold the modern Olympic Games

26.What famously happened to the Titanic in 1912?

A.   It sunk
B.   It caught on fire
C.   It blew up
D.   It was built

Answer: A, In 1912, the Titanic hit an iceberg and sank

27. What is the name of the building where the United States president lives?

A.   Blue House
B.   Red House
C.   White House
D.   Big House

Answer: C, The White House is where the US president lives

28. Where can the famous building - the Empire State Building - be found?

A.   Atlanta
B.   Los Angeles
C.   Dallas
D.   New York

Answer: D, The Empire State Building is located in New York

29. What do the stars on the US flag represent?

A.   The cities in the USA
B.   The states in the USA
C.   The rivers in the USA
D.   The mountains in the USA

Answer: B, The stars on the American flag represent the different states in the USA.

30. Who Wrote the most prolific plays of all time, Such as Hamlet, Macbeth, Othello?

A.   Edgar Allen Poe
B.   Robert Frost
C.   William Shakespeare
D.   Ludwig Van Beethoven

Answer: C, William Shakespeare wrote Hamlet, Macbeth, Othello and many others.

31. What is the famous prison called in California located on an island, surrounded by water?

A.   Federal Correctional Complex
B.   United States Penitentiary
C.   Alcatraz

D.   Gulags

Answer: C, Alcatraz was built off the coast of San Francisco in 1968.

SCIENCE AND NATURE TRIVIA

"There is no better designer than nature." - Alexander Mcqueen

1. Our atmosphere is kept wrapped around the Earth by a:

A.   Moving weather pattern
B.   Magnetic field
C.   Constant pressure from space
D.   Gravitational pull

Answer: B, The atmosphere is kept close to the earth by a magnetic field

2. Most places on Earth experience:

A.   Droughts
B.   Excessive winds
C.   Rainy seasons

D.   Four seasons

Answer: D, Most places on earth experience four seasons

3. What percentage of earth is covered in water?

A.   20%
B.   30%
C.   70%
D.   100%

Answer: C, 70% of our earth is covered in water with land only accounting for the other 30%

4. In our solar system, earth is the _____ planet from our sun.

A.   2nd
B.   1st
C.   6th
D.   5th

Answer: D, earth is the 5th planet from our sun

5. What can be found on earth that no other planet in our solar system possesses?

A.   Water
B.   Seasons
C.   Sunlight
D.   Life

Answer: D, Life make our planet unique from the rest

6. Earth is the _____ largest planet in our solar system.

A.   2nd
B.   9th
C.   5th
D.   10th

Answer: C, Earth is the 5th largest planet in our solar system

7. What are the two main metals in the earth's core?

A.   Gold and silver
B.   Silver and iron
C.   Iron and platinum

D.   Iron and nickel

Answer: D, Iron and nickel are the two main metals found in earths core

8. What do you call a person who studies rocks?

A.   Geologist
B.   Meteorologist
C.   Rockologist
D.   Zoologist

Answer: A, a geologist studies rocks

9. What part of the plant conducts photosynthesis?

A.   Trunk
B.   Flower
C.   Leaf
D.   Branch

Answer: C, The leaf conducts photosynthesis

10. What is the boiling point of water?

A.   25 degrees Celsius
B.   100 degrees Celsius
C.   0 degrees Celsius
D.   70 degrees Celsius

Answer: B, 100 degrees Celsius is the boiling point of water

11. What body part helps pump blood throughout the body?

A.   Brain
B.   Heart
C.   Lungs
D.   Liver

Answer: B, The heart is the pump within your body when it comes to blood!

12. The three states of matter are solid, liquid and
_____

A.   Fire
B.   Water
C.   Gas

D.   Heat

Answer: C, Gas is the last possible state for matter to be found in

13. What does boiling water turn into?

A.   Snow
B.   Clouds
C.   Mist
D.   Steam

Answer: D, boiling water turns into steam

14. What group of animals have scales on their bodies?

A.   Reptiles
B.   Amphibians
C.   Mammals
D.   Humans

Answer: A, Reptiles have scales on them

15. What nutrient is the source of muscle building?

A.   Carbohydrates
B.   Fiber
C.   Protein
D.   Sugar

Answer: C, Proteins help us build muscle

16. What gas do plants need in order to perform photosynthesis?

A.   Carbon dioxide
B.   Oxygen
C.   Ammonia
D.   Carbon monoxide

Answer: A, Carbon dioxide is what plants need in order to perform photosynthesis

17. What are the layers of gases that surround the earth called?

A.   Ozone
B.   Hydrosphere
C.   Atmosphere
D.   Omnisphere

Answer: C, The atmosphere surrounds the earth

18. What do similar blood cells form when they group together?

A.   Tissues
B.   Organs
C.   Bone
D.   Teeth

Answer: A, When blood cells group together they form tissues.

19. When animals eat both plants and meat, what are they called?

A.   Vegetarians
B.   Herbivores
C.   Omnivores
D.   Carnivores

Answer: C, Omnivores feast on anything from plants to other animals

20. Biology is the study of what?

A.   Earth
B.   Living things
C.   Plants
D.   Dead things

Answer: B, Biologists study plants, animals, and anything that is alive in the universe.

21. What are considered the basic building blocks of all living things?

A.   Cells
B.   Atoms
C.   Electrons
D.   Organisms

Answer: A, All living things are made up of one or more cells.

22. Which of the following is most responsible for the weather on earth?

A.   The ocean
B.   The sun
C.   The moon

D.   Global warming

Answer: D, Even though the sun is far away, it's heat gives Earth's atmosphere the energy to move, creating weather

23. Which of the following is NOT a layer of the Earth?

A.   Mantle
B.   Crust
C.   Inner Core
D.   Plate

Answer: D, The Earth's layers include the core, mantle, outer core, and inner core

24. What galaxy do we live in?

A.   Black eye galaxy
B.   Cartwheel galaxy
C.   Milky Way Galaxy
D.   Oreo Galaxy

Answer: C, our solar system is a part of the Milky Way Galaxy

25. What are igneous rocks made out of?

A.   Smaller rocks
B.   Salt
C.   Crystals
D.   Sand

Answer: C, Igneous rocks form when magma cools and crystalizes.

26. Which of the following is NOT part of the scientific method?

A.   Experimentation
B.   Dependent Variable
C.   Manipulation
D.   Hypothesis

Answer: D, The scientific method steps are: Question, Research, Hypothesis,

Experiment, Collect Data, Analysis, Conclusion.

27. What is yeast?

A.   A plant
B.   An animal
C.   A bacterium
D.   A fungus

Answer: D, Yeast is a type of fungus

28. A single piece of DNA is called what?

A.   Chromosome
B.   Nucleus
C.   Ribosome
D.   Cytoplasm

Answer: A, A single piece of DNA is called a chromosome

29. What was once considered a planet in our solar system but is now considered a dwarf planet?

A.   Venus
B.   Pluto
C.   Centauri b
D.   Jupiter

Answer: B, Pluto was once considered a full-sized planet but it now considered a dwarf planet.

30. What system of the body controls the senses?

A.   Circulatory system
B.   Nervous system
C.   Skeletal system
D.   Digestive system

Answer: B, the nervous system controls the senses within the body.

31. How many colors are rainbows comprised of?

A.   4
B.   3
C.   2
D.   7

Answer: D, Rainbows have 7 colors: red, orange, yellow, green, blue, indigo, violet.

SPORTS TRIVIA

"Sports do not build character; they reveal it" - John Woode

    1.   In what sport is the word 'love' used?

A.   Ice hockey
B.   Basketball
C.   Tennis
D.   Baseball

Answer: C, tennis used the word love is used to describe a players points.

2. What type of race is the Tour de France?

A.   Running
B.   Biking
C.   Walking
D.   Swimming

Answer: B, The Tour de France is a biking race

3. What is Canada's national winter sport?

A.   Ice hockey
B.   Volleyball
C.   Lacrosse
D.   Soccer

Answer: A, Ice hockey is Canada's national winter sport

4. What is the name of the championship series that the National Basketball Association has to end the playoffs?

A.   NBA Finals
B.   World basketball series
C.   World basketball championship
D.   NBA Playoffs

Answer: A, The championship in the NBA is called the NBA Finals

5. Which golf club is used when players want to hit the

ball as far as possible?

A.   Sand Wedge
B.   Iron
C.   Putter
D.   Driver

Answer: D, A driver is used to hit a golf ball as far as possible

6. What is the area called where baseball players watch their team play from?

A.   Den
B.   Bullpen
C.   Stands
D.   Dugout

Answer: D, Baseball players watch their fellow teammates play from the dugout

7. What is soccer's international championship games called?

A.   Global Football Championship

B.   Soccer Playoffs
C.   World Cup
D.   World Series

Answer: C, The international soccer championship games is called the World Cup

8. How many periods are in an ice hockey game?

A.   2
B.   3
C.   1
D.   4

Answer: B, Ice hockey is made up of 3 periods. However, at the NHL level, if both teams are tied at the end of the 3rd period, the game will go into a 4th period called 'overtime'.

9. In football, what is the name of the trophy that the Super Bowl winners receive?

A.   Stanley Cup
B.   Vince Lombardi Trophy
C.   Grey Cup
D.   NFL Cup

Answer: B, The name of the trophy is called Vince Lombardi Trophy which was first awarded in 1967.

10. What sport was Michael Jordan famous for?

A.   Basketball
B.   Football
C.   Baseball
D.   Cricket

Answer: A, Michael Jordan was famous for basketball. However, he did try his hand at baseball as well but never really made a name for himself in that sport.

11. What sport did Michael Phelps compete in during the Olympic games?

A.   Ice hockey
B.   Swimming
C.   Table tennis
D.   Track & Field

Answer: B, Michael Phelps competed in swimming events over his Olympic career.

12. Where would you see a pommel horse?

A.   Horseback riding
B.   Cricket
C.   Gymnastics
D.   Tennis

Answer: C, gymnastics use a pommel horse.

13. A caddie carries around a bag for what types of athlete?

A.   A golfer
B.   A cricket player
C.   A field hockey player
D.   A water polo player

Answer: A, golfers have assistants called caddies who carry their golf club bags for them and help them with decisions on shots.

14. How many pins do you have to knock down to get a strike in bowling?

A.   8

B.   10
C.   12
D.   6

Answer: B, you have to knock down 10 pins in bowling to get a strike.

15. Of these 4 answers, which one is NOT a golf term?

A.   Home Run
B.   Birdie
C.   Bogey
D.   Par

Answer: A, a home run is a term used in Baseball and cricket when a player hits a ball out of the playing area.

16. If you throw a strike, make a spare or throw a gutter ball, you are playing what sport?

A.   Bowling
B.   Basketball
C.   Golf
D.   Track & Field

Answer: A, the terms gutter ball, spare and strike are all

from the sport bowling

17. What do you put on the end of your cue stick in order to ensure you make clean contact with the cue ball?

A.   Water
B.   Tar
C.   Oil
D.   Chalk

Answer: D, chalk is used on the ends of cue sticks in order to make sure the cue ball and it have clean contact

18. Which of these sports does not use a net?

A.   Soccer
B.   Golf
C.   Tennis
D.   Volleyball

Answer: B, golf does not use nets unlike the other sports from that question.

19. What is the name of the playing area in which boxing matches are held?

A.   Diamond
B.   Field
C.   Court
D.   Ring

Answer: D, boxers fight in an area called 'the ring'.

20. Crawl, backstroke and butterfly are different methods in which sport?

A.   Track & field
B.   Swimming
C.   Water polo
D.   Skiing

Answer: B, Swimming uses these terms as they are methods of swimming lengths in the pool.

21. Which sport uses the term slam dunk?

A.   Baseball
B.   Wrestling
C.   Basketball
D.   Darts

Answer: C, Basketball uses the term slam dunk for when a player jumps and slams the ball through the hoop of the basketball net.

22. Dump, floater and wipe are terms used in which team sport?

A.   Basketball
B.   Biking
C.   Rock Skipping
D.   Volleyball

Answer: D, Volleyball utilizes the terms dump, floater and wipe

23. A tennis game with one player on each side is called?

A.   A singles match
B.   A doubles match
C.   A two person
D.   Head on match

Answer: A, a tennis match with one player on each side is called a singles match.

24. In NASCAR, what does the term "groove" mean?

A.   Getting fresh tires
B.   Practice of racing nose to tail
C.   Strategy of pitting week before running out
D.   Best route around the track

Answer: D, "Groove" is a slang term for the best route around the racetrack. The "high groove" takes a car close to the outside wall, while the "low groove" stays closer to the apron.

25. In golf, what do you call a score of 4 under par on any given hole?

A.   A pelican
B.   An eagle
C.   A condor
D.   A turkey

Answer: C, A "condor" is the name for a score of 4 under par.

26. Whose ear did Mike Tyson bite off during a 1997 boxing match?

A.   Buster Douglas
B.   Evander Holyfield
C.   Lennox lewis
D.   Floyd Mayweather

Answer: B, During his fight against Evander Holyfield in 1997, Mike Tyson was disqualified after biting off part of Holyfield's ear.

27. What sport uses a broom?

A.   Slamball
B.   Cricket
C.   Wakeboarding
D.   Curling

Answer: D, Curling uses a broom to sweep the ice surface in the path of the stone to speed it up or slow it down.

28. Squash is a member of which sport family?

A.   Football
B.   Running sports
C.   Water sports
D.   Racket sports

Answer: D, Squash is a racket sport played in a four-walled court with a small, hollow rubber ball.

29. What sports league awards the Art Ross trophy to the player who leads the league in points?

A.   National Hockey League
B.   Major League of Soccer
C.   National Basketball Association
D.   National Football League

Answer: A, The Art Ross Trophy is awarded to the National Hockey League (NHL) player who leads the league in points at the end of the regular season.

30. What player was nicknamed "Mr. Hockey"?

A.   Mark Messier
B.   Gordie Howe
C.   Bobby Orr
D.   Wayne Gretsky

Answer: B, Nicknamed "Mr. Hockey", Gordie Howe is considered the most complete player to ever play the game and one of the greatest ice hockey players of all time.

MATH TRIVIA

1. What descriptions best suits the characteristics of a rectangle?

A.   Equal on all sides
B.   Round on all sides and no 90 degree angles
C.   2 sides of equal length and two shorter sides of equal length
D.   3 sides in total

Answer: C, A rectangle has 2 sides of equal length and two shorter sides of equal length.

2. What is the next prime number after 7?

A.   8
B.   11
C.   9
D.   12

Answer: B, 11 is the next prime number after 7.

3. How many eggs would you have if you bought half a dozen?

A.   4
B.   5
C.   6
D.   12

Answer: C, a traditional dozen is equal to 12, so, half a dozen would be 6 since 6 is half of 12.

4. How many textbooks are on a bus of 20 children with 5 textbooks each?

A.   60 textbooks
B.   100 textbooks
C.   150 textbooks
D.   20 textbooks

Answer: B, 100 textbooks would be on the bus since 20 times 5 equals 100!

5. If an item costs $2.00 and there's a "buy four get one

free" sale on it, how much do four cost?

A. $10.00
B. $8.00
C. $12.00
D. $6.00

Answer: D, since the 4th one is free, you would times 2 by 3 and you get $6.00.

6. If 1GB of memory can hold 350 songs, how many songs can 2GB of memory hold?

A.   500
B.   700
C.   1000
D.   600

Answer: B, Since 350 times 2 equals 700

7. What would you get back for change on a $4.52 purchase if you paid with a $5 bill?

A.   50 cents
B.   1 dollar

C.   48 cents
D.   1 dollar 48 cents

Answer: C, since $5.00 minus $4.52 equals $0.48.

8. If Joan buys a candy bar for $0.50 every day, how much will she spend with candy in 2 weeks?

A. $6
B. $14
C. $12
D. $7

Answer: D, since 14 days (which is 2 weeks) times 0.50 equals 7!

9. How many cookies should be given to each of 9 children to evenly share a box of 27?

A.   3
B.   5
C.   4
D.   10

Answer: A, 3 cookies would be given to each child since 27 divided by 9 equals 3

10. If the teacher has 28 students in her class, how many are absent if only 23 chairs are filled?

A.   28
B.   23
C.   5
D.   7

Answer: C, there would be 5 students missing since 28 total students minus 23 full chairs equals 5 students missing.

11. In math, what does the word "sum" mean?

A.   Multiplication
B.   Division
C.   Addition
D.   Subtraction

Answer: C, Sum means the answer to an addition problem

12. In math, what does the word "minus" mean?

A.   Addition
B.   Subtraction
C.   Multiplication
D.   Division

Answer: B, Minus refers to the act of subtracting a number from another number

13. If Max has $50 and each shirt costs $10, how many shirts can Max buy?

A.   10
B.   5
C.   7
D.   15

Answer: B, Since 50 divided by 10 equals 5, that means Max can buy 5 shirts!

14. What is the top number of a fraction called?

A.   Numerator
B.   Denominator
C.   Top Number
D.   Instigator

Answer: A, the top number of a fraction is called the numerator

15. What is a shape with 8 sides called?

A.   Hexagon
B.   Polygon
C.   Octagon
D.   Square

Answer: C, an octagon, since 'octa' means 8

16. What is the next prime number after 3?

A.   7
B.   11
C.   15
D.   5

Answer: D, 5 is the next prime number after 3

17. What does the term 'century' represent?

A.   10 years
B.   100 years
C.   1000 years
D.   5000 years

Answer: B, A century represent 100 consecutive years

18. What are integers?

A.   Odd Numbers
B.   Even numbers
C.   Do not include fractions
D.   Are fractions

Answers: C, Integers are similar to whole numbers and also include negative numbers, but do not include fractions

19. What is the sum of the angles of a triangle?

A.   90 degrees
B.   200 degrees
C.   180 degrees
D.   300 degrees

Answer: C, 180 degrees is the sum of all angles of a

triangle

20. What do you call a triangle with different sides?

A.   Scalene triangle
B.   Isosceles triangle
C.   Acute
D.   Equilateral

Answer: A, A triangle with different sides is called a scalene triangle.

21. Which polygon has the least number of sides?

A.   Square
B.   Quadrilateral
C.   Triangle
D.   Octagon

Answer: C, A triangle has the least amount of sides of all polygons with only 3 sides.

22. How many points are there on a pentagon?

A.   3
B.   2
C.   8
D.   5

Answer: D, There are 5 sides on a pentagon. 'Penta' means 5.

23. The perimeter of a circle is also known as what?

A.   Circumference
B.   Polynomial
C.   Radius
D.   Length

Answer: A, The perimeter of a circle is also known as circumference

25. John has 21 apples and needs to divide them amongst 7 people evenly. How many apples will each person get?

A.   5
B.   3
C.   2
D.   1

Answer: B, 3 apples would go to each person because 21 divided by 7 equals 3.

26. Lucas has $27. He spent $7 at the corner store and another $10 on a t-shirt. How much money does Lucas have left over?

A. $5
B. $7
C. $11
D. $10

Answer: D, Lucas has $10 left over since $27 minus $7 equals $20 and then another $10 minus $20 equals $10.

27. If Alex drove north 50 kilometers, then drove south 10 kilometers and then drove north another 20 kilometers, how far did he end up going?

A.   60 kilometers
B.   40 kilometers
C.   80 kilometers
D.   100 kilometers

Answer: A, 60 kilometers would be the total distance Alex drove.

28. The term 'product' refers to what form of math?

A.   Substraction
B.   Addition
C.   Multiplication
D.   Division

Answer: C, the answer to a multiplication problem is called the product.

29. How many faces does a cube have?

A.   2
B.   4
C.   6
D.   8

Answer: C, a cube has 6 different faces in total

30. What are the corners of a shape also known as?

A.   Faces
B.   Angles

C. Edges

D. Vertices

Answer: D, The corners of a shape can also be called 'Vertices'.

CONCLUSION

Wow! You made it through all of the trivia and multiple choice questions in *Trivia for Smart Kids*. How did you end up doing? These trivia questions are some of our personal favorites and have had huge impacts on people all around the world. We hope they had the same effect on you!

Once again, we would like to thank you for reading our book *Trivia for Smart Kids* and can't wait to hear what you thought about it. If you enjoyed listening to this book, please don't forget to leave a review and let us know how much you loved it. Reviews mean the world to us and help us continue to create books just like this one for years to come.

Keep an eye out for Trivia For Smart Kids Part 2!

Thank you!

DL Digital Entertainment

Lightning Source UK Ltd.
Milton Keynes UK
UKHW020955270420
362295UK00001B/1

9 781989 777558